DREAMS

THE HIDDEN MEANING AND INTERPRETATIONS BEHIND YOUR DREAMS

Victoria Lane

Relentless Progress Publishing

© 2015

TABLE OF CONTENTS

YOUR FREE GIFT

As a special Thank You for downloading this book I have put together an exclusive special report on the life changing **Superfoods** that I believe can help anybody.

Are you tired of feeling *sluggish, overweight*, and *unhappy*? Odds are you are eating the Standard American Diet (SAD) and not getting enough of the nutrients and vitamins that keep our bodies and minds operating at peak levels.

Enter *"Superfoods - The 12 Top Healing Superfoods to Live Longer, Look Younger, and Feel Amazing"*

In this free lengthy report of over 10,000 words you will learn about the top 12 readily available Superfoods you need to be using to help you look younger, ward off disease, and lose weight.

>>You can Download this Free Report by Clicking Here<<

>>awesomehabits.com/superfoodsbook<<

A BRIEF HISTORY OF DREAM INTERPRETATION

We know that humans as well as certain animals dream almost every night. The difference here is that humans have always been fascinated by their dreams and have therefore made substantial effort to understand the hidden meaning behind these dreams.

Dream interpretation, also referred to as dream analysis, is based on the idea that you can attach meaning to your dreams.

IS THIS USEFUL?

Well, the process of dream analysis has been used in a wide variety of settings. These include various religions and ancient civilizations. In fact, the curiosity behind the hidden meaning of our dreams is what leads us to a bookstore and search for a book on dream analysis.

People in the ancient civilizations looked at dreaming as a way to communicate with people around them or even with the Gods. Some of these civilizations include the Egyptians and the Babylonians. People in ancient Egypt valued the process of dream interpretation – they saw it as a means to foretell the future, heal from within, cure sickness and of course, initiate a dialogue with God. The Egyptian civilization even had a God and Goddess of dreams who would help them in analyzing and interpreting their dreams. Earlier, this method of communication with the Gods, was looked at as being supernatural – it was often considered a divine intervention. Hence, the process of dream interpretation was limited to people who were blessed with supernatural powers.

Around the time, 3000-4000 B.C. dreams were documented on clay tablets.

In certain primitive societies, people developed an ability to distinguish between the dream world and the waking world. Sometimes, they consciously chose not to make that distinction. Most people saw the dream world as not only an extension of reality, but as a much more powerful world – powerful than reality itself!

The Greeks and the Romans viewed dreams in a religious context. According to them, dreams were direct messages from the dead or the Gods. Very often, dreams were looked upon as solution providers – they helped people decide on the actions that they should or should not take. People believed that dreams forewarned them about the bad things that could happen, they helped in predicting the future and even provided solutions on how to avoid any mishappenings.

People constructed special shrines where they could sleep with hope that they would receive a message from God or a solution to their problems through their dreams. Dreams even dictated the actions of great military leaders and political strategists – that was the power they held. In fact, a number of military leaders took dream interpreters along with them into the battle. These interpreters helped these leaders with the war strategy.

Aristotle, the Greek philosopher, believed that specific physiological functions led to dreams. This could help in diagnosis of illness and even predict onset of certain diseases.

If we go back to the Hellenistic period, we will learn that the main purpose behind dream interpretation was centered on its ability to heal. A number of temples were especially constructed keeping in mind the healing power of dreams. These temples were called as the Asclepieions and the popular belief at that time was that sick people who slept in these temples would be sent cures through the Divine power via their dreams. Doctors also used dream interpreters, who helped them in making a clear diagnosis. Dreams offered certain definite clues that provided an idea to the healer about the potential disorder that the sufferer was facing.

Certain priests acted as dream interpreters in Ancient Egypt. The Egyptians recorded their dreams in symbols or pictographs. In fact, it was believed that people who dreamt certain significant, specific and vibrant dreams were special as they were directly blessed by God. Somebody who possessed the power of dream interpretation was considered as specially and divinely gifted.

Some people looked at dreams as a place that your soul and spirit would visit every night. According to the Chinese philosophy, the soul leaves the human body to enter the dream world. They also believed that abrupt waking up prevents the soul from returning to the human body. This is reason why the Chinese are still cautious of alarm clocks.

A number of Mexican and Native American civilizations believed that their ancestors visited them through their dreams. They believed that these ancestors would sometimes take on non-living forms such as stones, rocks or plants. Therefore, dreams were seen as a mechanism to establish contact with ancestors and also a method that helps in assigning a purpose to life.

People in the Middle Ages viewed dreams as something evil and looked at its images as temptations from the devil. It was said that the devil fills the human mind with poisonous thoughts when it is most vulnerable – that is when it is in a sleep state. This would mislead humans to follow an incorrect path.

People in the nineteenth century dismissed dreams as pictures stemming out of anxiety, tension, stress, indigestion and noise. This also meant that there was no real meaning attached to dreams and this naturally killed the desire to interpret dreams.

However, in the late nineteenth century, Sigmund Freud revolutionized the study of dreams and therefore, revived the need for dream interpretation, stunning the world of psychiatry.

If we trace back to ancient civilizations, almost all evidences point towards the fact that people had a great inclination to interpret dreams. The holy Bible, has at least seven hundred references to dreams.

UNDERSTANDING THE HOW AND WHY OF DREAMING

It is important to understand the role dreams play in our lives. Before we get to analyzing and interpreting our dreams, we must understand the psychological and the physical role that dreams play in our lives.

Let us first take a closer look at the **sleep cycle**:

There are four stages in the sleep cycle. Dreams normally occur in the REM stage, however, this is not a rule carved in stone. Some people also dream during the other stages of sleep, however, it is safe to say that the dreams occurring during the REM sleep cycle are the most memorable ones. The complete sleep cycle (including the four stages) lasts for around 90-120 minutes, depending on the individual. This also implies that an average person experiences approximately four to eight sleep cycles in his regular eight to nine hour of sleep time.

Stage1: This is called the REM stage or the Rapid Eye Movement stage. During this stage, your eyes erratically and rapidly move back and forth. This typically occurs 90-100 minutes after you have slept and this is the time when dreams are most memorable.

Stage 2: REM is followed by the cycle of light sleep. This is the stage where you experience non rapid eye movements. Your heart rate slows down and muscles are completely relaxed. This is the stage when you are preparing for deep sleep.

Stage 3 and 4: These are the two stages when your body enters the deep sleep cycle. It completely gives in to deep sleep and you do experience some non-rapid eye movements.

The important thing to understand here is that these four cycles repeat themselves over and over again for at least five to seven times during one night. The most memorable dreams occur during stage one or the REM stage.

Research proves that humans do dream in other stages of sleep as well, however, they may not remember those dreams.

UNDERSTANDING THE PSYCHOLOGICAL ASPECT OF DREAMING:

Science does not fully understand the aspect of dream sleep. However, there are several studies that suggest how deprivation of dream sleep leads to definite psychological impact.

A study conducted to look at the impact of dreaming had volunteers who achieved the same amount of sleep but were awakened right before their REM cycle (or the dream sleep cycle) kicked in. These volunteers were then left to sleep again. They were awakened again before the commencement of their dream sleep cycle. This process continued the entire night. Overall, they were allowed to sleep for the same amount of time as they normally did.

It was observed that the volunteers reported feelings of disorientation, depression, anger, stress and other psychological symptoms during the day. When this study was repeated for several nights, it resulted in a marked elevation in psychological symptoms.

This proved that although sleep is extremely important for a person's health and overall well-being, dreams are equally important too.

UNDERSTANDING THE PHYSICAL ASPECT OF DREAMING:

The study of brain waves during dream sleep reveals important physical changes that occur in a person's body during this time. These include an elevated level of adrenaline along with an increase in the blood pressure and heart rate. In fact, research proves that the activities in the brain are higher in dream sleep than in waking hours. If we keep that in mind, we can look at dreaming as a higher state of consciousness.

Dream sleep is also called the Rapid Eye Movement sleep or the REM sleep. This is because as the person dreams, even though his eyes are closed, they move rapidly underneath the eyelids. This process occurs in the final stages of a person's sleep and constitutes around twenty percent of the person's total sleep time.

An average person may dream around five to seven times, however, they usually remember only the dreams that they dreamt close to their waking time.

Sometimes, people do not remember any dreams. This does not imply that these people did not dream – almost everybody dreams every night. Dreams typically kick off thirty to ninety minutes after falling asleep. As a person attains the deepest state of sleep, the REM cycle begins to repeat. This repeats a number of times during one single night.

During REM sleep, specific changes are observed in a person's blood pressure and heart rate.

Another important point to be remembered is that during dream sleep, your body is completely immobile. You may twist and turn in other stages of sleep, however, during the REM cycle, your muscles are totally relaxed and you do not move.

A number of researchers also refer to this state as 'dream paralysis' or 'sleep paralysis.'

THE BEGINNER FAQ'S TO DREAMING

Most dreamers have a very basic question in their mind – Why do they dream and if there is any significance attached to their dreams?

Now, dreams are unique to each person. The interpretation of dreams, therefore, is also unique!

The world of dream interpretation is vivid, rich, exciting and baffling.

Here are a few questions that most beginners ask when they get started with dream interpretation:

DO DREAMS HAVE ANY SIGNIFICANCE?

Well, when you interpret dreams, you normally use a symbolic language. Most of the images that are investigated have a hidden meaning and a definite interpretation. Hence, dreams cannot be viewed as a common reality and interpretation – as this will differ depending on the profile and situation of the dreamer. All dreams must be looked upon as symbolic representation of something bigger.

WHAT IS THE AVERAGE NUMBER OF DREAMS PEOPLE HAVE IN A NIGHT?

An average dreamer normally has anything between four to seven dreams in a night. They normally spend around two to three hours in their dream sleep.

WHY DO PEOPLE SOMETIMES EXPERIENCE RECURRING DREAMS?

Recurring dreams are the most common types of dreams. They suggest that the dreamer has certain specific issues during the waking life and these may need immediate attention. The dreamer must spend some time analyzing the root cause of these recurring dreams. Only then will he be able to put the power of dream interpretation to good use.

DO PEOPLE DREAM EVERY NIGHT?

Yes, people dream every night. The main challenge is remembering these dreams. The dreams closest to your sleep cycle are the most memorable ones.

WHAT IS THE AVERAGE DURATION OF A DREAM?

On an average, a dream lasts between ten to twenty minutes per session of the dream sleep cycle.

Do animals also dream?

Research proves that mammals demonstrate similar brain activity as humans. It can therefore be presumed that animals do dream. However, what they dream is still a mystery.

Does color have any significance in dream analysis?

Most people dream in color, however, they do not notice the difference between various colors during their natural dream sleep. This is because humans deal with a lot of color in their daily life. This makes them sometimes overlook the importance of color in their dreams. The sense of colors is one of the first things to fade from the conscious mind.

Does daily activity impact dreams?

It is said that sometimes certain thoughts and feelings are held back during the day. These are expressed at night through dreams. An example of this could be that you were angry during the day. However, you could not express your anger due to various reasons. Now, as you sleep during the night, your anger may manifest itself through your dreams. Have you heard of certain traumatic nightmares? These are cases of trauma patients who relive their experiences through their dreams.

Do children and adults dream about similar things and do these things have a definite meaning?

Unlike adults, children do not dream about themselves until the age of three. This is because they do not develop a sense of self before the age of three. However, if a child experiences trauma, it is likely that he or she would also experience nightmares. The frequency of nightmares is maximum between the age of three and eight.

I know I dream a lot, but I only seem to remember bad dreams. Are there any specific reasons for this?

Well, your brain is naturally wired to remember the most vivid experiences. Since bad dreams also constitute vivid experiences, it is only natural to remember them more than the good ones. Sometimes, bad dreams wake you up from REM sleep. This ensures that you remember them even more.

I GUESS I DON'T REMEMBER MY DREAMS BECAUSE I WAS SNORING.

No, that is not true! You would most probably remember the dreams that you dream about closer to your wake up time. Snoring and dreaming never happen simultaneously.

DO MEN AND WOMEN DREAM IN A DIFFERENT MANNER?

If we were to analyze the brain wave activity during REM sleep for men and women, we would notice that it is similar for both men and women. The content of dreams may vary for men and women. Women tend to dream about men and women both and men generally tend to dream about other men. Isn't that a revelation?

I HAVE HEARD THAT HITTING THE GROUND DURING A FALLING DREAM MEANS THAT I WILL DIE. IS IT TRUE?

A number of times, dreams of falling or hitting the ground wake up the dreamer from sleep. You must, however, understand that these kind of dreams are not at all a terminal experience. In fact, they have been shared by a number of dreamers.

I DREAM ABOUT DREAMING. IS IT NORMAL?

To dream about dreaming is perfectly normal. It simply implies that the dreamer has to deal with issues related to the subconscious mind. If this happens, the dreamer rarely wakes up prematurely and gets the time to confront and reflect on certain critical issues.

YES, IT IS IMPORTANT TO REMEMBER AND RECORD YOUR DREAMS!

Well, we all know that the science of dream interpretation has been around since the time we began to dream. The clay tablets that existed during 3000-4000 B.C. have a mention of dreams and their interpretation. This also implies that dream interpretation has been around since 6000 years approximately.

People use dream interpretation for various purposes – they can be fun, hobby or sometimes a full time career. A number of people have drawn benefit from the meaning dreams give to their lives.

The analysis of dreams continues to amaze people. However, before dreams can be analyzed, it is important to remember and record them. No interpretation can take place without appropriately remembering and recording these dreams. Hence, every effort must be made to remember them before they fade away.

In case you are looking at interpreting a dream, it is extremely important to capture it in writing. This implies that your dream journal must be kept as close to your bed as possible. In other words, it must be handy and accessible.

Another habit that you could develop is the habit of replaying your dreams. You must replay your dreams in your mind before you open your eyes in the morning. When you do this, you reinforce the minutest detail present in your dream – you may forget this detail otherwise.

Now, when you write down these dreams, write down the minutest possible details. You need to write down every single thing – even if it is simply a hazy phrase. Your only goal here is to capture your dream to the minutest possible level.

When you have everything jotted down, take some time to read your dreams and fill in as much gaps as you can. During this process, you must highlight any symbols or key phrases that you feel hold relevance to your real life.

Record your dreams in your dream journal every single day. This will help you spot any common patterns or key phrases that you believe have something to do with your daily life. If you notice that you have recurrent dreams, you can use the patterns for analysis and determination of the root cause.

I would suggest that you utilize the art and science of dream interpretation as a fun thing to do or a spare time hobby. The more serious stuff such as using dream interpretation for healing can be left for the professional healers.

An example of this could be you solely focusing on the symbolism in your dreams and utilizing it to analyze and interpret. Have you been recurrently dreaming about being naked? This could relate to symbolism of your secrets getting exposed. What you need to do in this case is examine yourself and look at those hidden secrets.

Have you been dreaming about falling from the ceiling? This could just mean that you or the situation that you are in is currently out of control. You might want to take a close look at your life to review the things that you can get in control.

THE VARIOUS TYPES OF DREAMS

The art and science of dream interpretation is a really fertile ground and almost everybody, including newbie learners, hobbyists and serious experts can get tangled in this ground. This is because dreams have no boundaries – they vary by subject and can cover almost everything that occurs in a person's waking life.

Here are some common types of dreams that dream researchers recognize:

THE DAYDREAM:

Daydreaming is not the conventional REM dream sleep kind of dreaming. As the name suggests, this occurs during the day or when you are awake. This may mean that when you daydream, you are in a state of consciousness – this may be the state between your being fully awake and fully asleep.

Research proves that most people spend around two hours of their time day dreaming. This is the time when you give wings to your imagination and begin to fly. You wander and move across exciting places and accomplish some beautiful things.

THE NIGHTMARE:

The first nightmare generally happens at the age of three and they continue till around six or seven. Children get to experience nightmares the most. Almost all normal people get to experience at least a few nightmares in their lifetime. People who have experienced extreme trauma generally dream vivid nightmares. This is their way to relieve that trauma. Nightmares are dealt with by professional psychologists and counselors.

THE LUCID DREAM:

Have you ever had dreams when you know that you are dreaming and wake up soon after the dream is over? Such dreams that provide you an awareness of dreaming and wake you up soon after they are over are termed as lucid dreams. Such individuals have developed control over the happenings of the dream world and are able to remain in the dream state till the time they have can exercise that control. Such dreamers enjoy the most exciting adventures night after night are often a dream researcher's most fascinating subject.

THE RECURRING DREAM:

As the name suggests, recurring dreams are dreams that repeat themselves. There could be instances when the same dream occurs night after night, at other instances – the details or scenario of the dream might change but the theme may remain unchanged. Such dreams are often associated with certain real life triggers but that may not be the case always. Some people experience recurring dreams in a soap opera fashion – this implies that their dreams pick off from the happenings of the night before. In such cases, the dreamer loves to and is generally anxious to go to sleep – simply because he wants to follow the story.

THE HEALING DREAM:

Some people experience healing dreams in which their body sends messages to the mind as they try and seek medical help. Such people are mostly spiritually inclined.

THE EPIC DREAM:

Sometimes, dreamers may experience dreams like a blockbuster movie. These dreams may remain fresh in the mind for months or years after the dream.

THE PROPHETIC DREAM:

Prophetic dreams are dreams where you dream about things that appear to come true in real life. Such dreams are mostly symbolic and seem to be difficult to identifiable as a prophecy or a coincidence. There may be various reasons for such dreams. Sometimes, your subconscious mind absorbs more information than your conscious mind – it then tries to rearrange this information during your dream sleep. Quite often, the subconscious mind picks up information or clues that lead to prediction of an event coming true.

MORE ABOUT DREAMS – THE IMAGERY

The science of dream interpretation begins with a basic understanding of dream colors and numbers. Through this chapter, we shall aim to understand the hidden meaning of numbers and colors that appear in your dreams.

UNDERSTANDING THE HIDDEN MEANING OF NUMBERS:

Numbers can be interpreted in a variety of ways and this depends on the context of your dream. And if you have ever had a chance to visit a numerologist, you would understand the vast and varied opinions they have about appearance of numbers in dreams. They might even suggest that you buy lottery tickets using the numbers that you see in your dreams.

Here are some common interpretations of numbers that appear in your dreams:

One: Dreaming about the number 'one' could simply mean unity or wholesomeness. This signifies that your life is complete.

Two: Dreaming about the number 'two' could signify balance and harmony in your life. This signifies that you have been successful or are aiming to achieve harmony and balance in your physical and spiritual world.

Three: Dreaming about the number 'three' signifies spiritual fulfilment. It is quite common to dream about the number 'three' and it depicts spiritual satisfaction and harmony.

Five: Dreaming about the number 'five' signifies an upcoming change. The manner in which this number appears in your dreams provides clues about this change and lets you know if you should welcome it or be prepared for it since it might be something that you fear.

UNDERSTANDING THE HIDDEN MEANING OF COLORS:

Sometimes, dreamers share that they dream in color and the shades are more intense than what they appear in the real world.

Here are some common interpretations of colors that appear in your dreams:

Pink: The color 'pink' is often linked with love. Dreaming in pink color may therefore imply an intense and happy love relationship.

Red: The color 'red' has two things associated with it – passion and anger. When you dream of a red object, it could imply passion or anger but will depend on the overall context of the dream.

Black: The color 'black' is associated with negativity and death. It may simply signify a large void in a person's life. Depending on the context, it may also mean fear of aging and death.

White: The color 'shite' represents purity. Depending on the context, 'white' may also mean fear of aging, death or simply fear of change.

Grey: The color 'grey' falls in between white and black. It also signifies fear or confusion. The interpretation is based on the context and may mean that the dreamer is struggling to find an answer.

Blue: Most people associate the color 'blue' to spirituality. However, some experts also take 'blue' as a feeling of sadness. The interpretation is based on the context of the dream.

Green: The color 'green' symbolizes prosperity, growth and renewal. Depending on the context, this may be associated with healing oneself, physically and spiritually. It may also mean growth, development and prosperity in business or relationships.

Yellow: The color 'yellow' is often referred to as the color of sunshine. This implies happiness and peace in the dreamer's life. Depending on the context, it may mean, hope, serenity and peace.

THINGS HAVE MEANING TOO!

It is common to dream about a house, kitchen, bathroom, eyes or may be the porch. Let us look at what this signifies:

Dreaming about eyes: Eyes are a most characteristic feature of a person's appearance. Therefore, it is only natural for a person to dream about eyes. Dreams about eyes may have various meanings. For example, seeing your eyes in mirror is a sign of knowledge, comprehension, understanding and sometimes spiritual enlightenment. It all depends on the context of the dream.

Eyes are considered a gateway to your soul. Sometimes, dreaming about eyes may mean hidden desires, wanting to break through. In certain contexts, it signifies subconscious thoughts trying to break free.

Sometimes, dreamers just see a single eye in their dreams. This also signifies various things, depending on the context. The right eye signifies the sun whereas the left eye is the symbol of the moon.

Seeing a single eye in your dream may also imply that you are a stubborn individual who does not care about other people's thoughts and emotions. Your judgment may be colored due to your own preconceived notions.

Sometimes, dreamers talk about dreaming about two eyes moving and turning around in their head. This is simply a sign of spiritual enlightenment. If you notice an inward turning of eyes in your dream, it signifies a desire to take a closer look at your life. This dream may signify a psychological turning point in your life.

Some dream experts argue that viewing a single eye or both eyes in your dreams is simply the Universe's way of letting you know that you need to take a closer look at your life. It is your subconscious asking you to trust your instincts, intuitions and examine your own self for answers.

Sometimes, you may dream about something getting into your eye. This implies that there is a roadblock or an obstacle in your life that now needs to be carefully removed. Some dream experts mention that this may imply that the dreamer is always critical about certain people or things.

Some people mention dreaming about the third eye.

Well, this may simply be a warning sign urging you to take a closer look at your inner self. In this case, you must listen to your inner vision.

If you are dreaming about injured eyes or impaired vision, it may simply imply that you are hesitant to face the truth. Depending on the context, this may also signify pain and hurt. It may also mean that you are trying to avoid intimacy and now must take another look at a particular relationship.

Have you ever dreamt about crossed eyes?

This implies that you are not seeing the true perspective and you are getting things mixed up.

Dreaming about houses: It is extremely common for people to dream about houses. The houses that you see in your dreams may be common or uncommon. Dream researchers and experts have classified these dreams based on the kind of room that you see in your dream. An example could be that you notice yourself moving into the basement. This would mean that you are going down into your life. Going into the attic, on the other hand may signify growth and development.

Let us try and examine the different rooms of your 'dream house':

The Attic: Viewing the attic in your dreams is definitely a sign of growth – physical as well as spiritual. Depending on the context, this may signify spiritual growth and enlightenment. It may also signify progress and development in your personal or professional life.

The Bathroom: If you are dreaming about the bathroom, you definitely possess an inner desire to be cleansed and healed. This could also signify the much awaited change that is required in your life. Sometimes, it just brings you closer to the mush awaited need to start afresh.

The Kitchen: The kitchen implies nourishment. Therefore, dreaming about the kitchen may just mean that your soul is waiting to be healed and nourished. For some people, this may mean the need for spiritual empowerment and nourishment. Dreams about kitchen are also interpreted keeping in view the state of the kitchen. What would it mean if you dream about a stocked up kitchen? It implies that you have achieved all that you wanted to and that your life is complete. An empty kitchen, on the other hand, may imply emptiness in your life, house or soul.

The Dining Room: The interpretation of dreaming about the dining room is similar to the interpretation of kitchen. Just like the kitchen, the dining room also provides nourishment to the person. However, when you dream about the dining room, it does signify that your need to get nourished is really urgent and must be dealt with immediately.

The Living Room: The living room is often linked to having a normal life. Dreaming about the living room implies interactions and relationships with other people, family and friends. The kind of work these relationships need is dependent on the context of the dream.

The Bedroom: Dreaming about the bedroom may signify various things – it may mean healthy sexual relationships, repressed sexuality, the need for rest, the need for love and care... and so on. It all depends on the context that you dream about the bedroom.

The Upstairs: If you dream about climbing the stairs, it may simply imply that you are searching for your higher self. It may also mean greater self- awareness and enlightenment.

The Downstairs: The basement or the downstairs can signify repressed desires or hidden feelings. If you dream about disturbing events in your basement, it could just mean that you are making an effort to come to terms with the disturbances in your life.

The Ground Floor: Dreaming about the ground floor signifies the happenings in your everyday life. This could mean happiness or grief depending on the context of the dream.

Visit to an old and familiar house: You may sometimes dream about visiting your childhood home. This may mean that you possess an internal longing to achieve happiness. Events such as a family reunion or a school meeting may trigger this longing and hence the dream.

The Hallway: Dreaming about the hallway signifies your need to explore hidden issues. It may also mean a new event or place in your life.

The Porch: You often dream about the porch when you are struggling to make a decision. Such dreams are therefore associated with indecisiveness or confusion.

INTERPRETING SOME COMMON DREAMS

This chapter aims to demystify some of the most common dreams.

DREAMING ABOUT ARMS

This is one of the most common dreams people dream of. They dream of arms – their own arms or somebody else's arms. Now, dreams about arms d not hold so much significance, but can be considered as significant if the dreamer clearly remembers the dreams. This is the reason a dream journal is always recommended.

If you see your own arms in your dream as a part of another dream story, it may imply our inner desire to care for and nurture others. This is most common if you are worried about another person. Sometimes, people dream about their arms reaching out. This signifies that they want to connect with other people in their lives.

Dreaming about arms may also represent struggles and challenges in your life. This will also vary according to the context in which you dream about these arms.

Some people dream about using their arms to defend themselves. This means that they need to protect themselves in their personal or professional lives. It may also signify a planned attack by another intruder and the need to guard your own self. Are you a little insecure at your place of work? In this scenario also, you may dream about using your arms to protect your own self.

An injured arm appearing in your dream may signify an inability to defend your own self. It may also imply feelings of helplessness or inability to care about others. Injured or broken arms may mean limitations or restrictions. The injury represents your lack of freedom.

Sometimes, the particular arm that you are dreaming about helps in interpreting your dream. Dreaming about the left arm is associated with femininity and therefore a desire to nurture and care. Dreaming about the right arm may signify masculinity and hence power. It may also imply an outgoing nature.

If you dream about injuring somebody's arm, it may just mean repressed anger. This signifies that you have not been able to express your anger when you needed to or may be helplessness in a particular situation.

DREAMING ABOUT TEETH

Sometimes people dream that their teeth are falling out. The teeth may fall with a light touch or simply crumble in the dreamer's hand. Such dreams are really frightening and hard to forget.

Dream experts have tried to explain the falling teeth through various theories. One theory mentions that dreaming about falling teeth signifies that you are immensely concerned about the way you look and the manner in which others perceive you. Since good looking teeth are an important part of your physical appearance, this theory seems to be valid. Losing teeth in sleep may depict your fear of losing your beauty. It may portray uncertainty and under-confidence. Losing teeth may also imply that you are having a tough time gaining attention from the opposite sex. They may also depict fear of aging or impotence.

Another theory links loss of teeth to embarrassment. This generally happens to people who fear public speaking. They may often dream about losing their teeth. This is similar to dreaming about being chased. It is recommended that the dreamer confronts his or her fears directly and tries to understand the root cause of embarrassment or anxiety.

Another theory associates teeth to power. We understand that the teeth have the power to bite, chew and tear. Losing teeth may therefore mean losing power or influence. Sometimes, people feel that their opinion is not valued. This leads to them seeing loss of teeth in their dreams. They feel powerless or helpless.

A number of menopausal women dream about losing their teeth. Here, the dream is simply a manifestation of fear to get old.

Certain dream interpreters believe that losing teeth in dreams may mean that the dreamer is putting his or her faith in man and is converting into an atheist. In this scenario, the Divine approaches the individual through their dreams and urges them to return to their Source or the Creator.

Dreams about losing teeth are interpreted differently across cultures – the Greeks view it as a warning about a friend or a family whereas the Chinese see this as a punishment for lying. Some cultures even associate money with missing teeth.

DREAMING ABOUT THE BACK

A number of dreamers mention that they dream about their or another person's back. If remembered in detail, these dreams can help you demystify some of the most important things in life.

The meaning of the dream depends on the context of the dream. In general, dreaming about the back refers to confidence, strength, burden, attitude and resilience.

If you dream about a hurting or a breaking back, it may simply mean that you are overwhelmed with the events in your life. Sometimes, the back is a symbol of external pressure and stress. This may translate to physical and psychological problems occurring in a person's life.

If you dream about a person turning their back towards you, it signifies that that particular person is either angry with you or jealous of you. In case you know who this person is, you may be able to work things out with him or her.

If you dream about fear of turning your back towards another person, it is a symbol of somebody backstabbing you or betraying you. Sometimes, people dream about friends and their own fear to turn their back towards their friends. This may signify a fear to lose a friend and this friend may not be the person you saw in your dreams.

It is common to view a naked back in your dreams. This signifies hidden secrets and your fear of getting exposed. It may also suggest that now is the time that you can come clean with confessions and reveal your secrets.

DREAMING ABOUT BEING CHASED

Dreaming about being chased signify fear of being caught. Such dreams seem to have originated during the time when our ancestors feared that they would get caught by predators. Now, even though there are no predators, the significance of dreams still remains the same – they signify the general fear in our lives. Such dreams are also linked to anxiety and tension. The manner in which you respond to general tension and anxiety greatly influences what you see in your dreams. Dreams about being chased are dreams about you experiencing loads of stress in your daily life. They depict how you want to run away from all the stress and fear that it may engulf you again. Such dreams can turn into nightmares if you do not address the situation immediately.

Sometimes, these dreams are a result of tasks that you have been procrastinating. You know you have to finish those tasks and therefore are engulfed by unnecessary stress.

Feelings of jealousy and anger may also lead to dreams about being chased.

Sometimes people gain mastery over their dreams and instead of running away from the situation, prefer to turn around and confront the attacker.

Women who live in places that have a high crime rate often dream about being chased. This may signify an inherent need to learn self-defense.

Whatever the reason for these dreams, the important part is understanding the root cause and ensuring that it is being addressed. It is best to confront your fears and bravely face them, instead of running away from the situation or person. Addressing the root cause can ensure that these chase dreams do not convert into nightmares and you enjoy a peaceful and restful sleep.

Chase dreams can sometimes occur as a reaction to a real life event. The main manifestation is that you are running away from the attacker. Feelings of stress, tension and anger can lead to such dreams. These are a way of your subconscious sending you some clear signals. Confront the cause and try to address the real issue.

DREAMING ABOUT BEING NAKED

This is another common worth investigating dream. Dreaming about being naked can be interpreted in different ways – depending upon the context in which it is being dreamt. Sometimes, it may simply signify the nakedness a person is going through in their daily lives. There may be occasions when only the dreamer is aware of this nakedness.

In some contexts, dreaming about being naked is associated with fear of exposure. This means that you are worried about certain secrets that may be uncovered. When it is just you who notices the nakedness, it implies that your fear is irrational and not based on anything.

Sometimes, a dreamer is dreaming about something and suddenly realizes that he or she is naked. This may signify guilt, fear and shame. It may also be representative of a secret that is about to be uncovered.

Dreaming about nakedness can also suggest fear of being caught. Clothes in dreams are often linked to concealment. Stripping yourself means that a big secret or something that you have been hiding is about to be uncovered. Being suddenly naked is linked to fear or lack of preparedness. You may not be prepared for an important event, an exam or a work meeting – it could be anything.

Sometimes, this dream may not be related to your real life. It may simply signify fear of being caught or exposed.

Though rare, sometimes the dreamer dreams about being naked and this may signify freedom instead of fear. This means that the dreamer has not secret to hide and therefore does not fear being caught off-guard. He or she is completely liberated from the fear.

Dreaming About Flying:

This is one of the most fascinating category to investigate. This is also sometimes referred to as the lucid dream.

Dreaming about flying is generally a pleasant experience for the dreamer and they link it to feelings of pleasure, joy and excitement.

Flying over a familiar landscape may suggest that you are in control of the situation and are feeling great about it. Since you are on the top of the situation, you also have the power to control the speed with which and the destination to which you want to travel.

If you dream about your inability to fly, it may suggest that in real life you are not in control of the situation. Such dreams also depict helplessness and powerlessness.

In case you dream about fear of flying, it depicts that you are scared to take on challenges in real life. It means that there is a lot of uncertainty surrounding you and fear difficult situations.

Trees and mountains that appear in your dreams during the process of flying are examples of real life obstacles. Your aim should be analyzing your current situation, looking at the barriers and dealing with them by confronting them.

Such dreams seem to fascinate the dream researchers more than the dreams about nakedness, eyes, arms or being chased. The reason for this is the dreamer's inability to fly in real life.

Flying may also signify a desire to do something better and greater than the present.

We understand that flying signifies power and wish to do something more than what you are currently doing. Lack of power may also manifest itself as a desire to fly in dreams.

Irrespective of the fact that it is positive or negative, this category of dreams seems to serve as the most fertile land in the big and fascinating world of dreams.

Dreaming About Falling

These dreams are extremely common and often lead to a person being suddenly awakened from their dream sleep.

There is another common misconception that makes people worry about these kinds of dreams unnecessarily. Most people believe that dreaming about falling is a symbol of death.

The fact is that dreaming about falling is associated with fear, anxiety, tension and stress in real life. In case you experience recurring dreams of falling, it may simply imply that you are overwhelmed in your day to day life and need some immediate solution.

Let me explain this with an example:

Let us talk about a dreamer who feels that his life is out of control and that he can do nothing to change the situation. In general, this person feels powerless and helpless in real life. It is quite possible that this person experiences dreams of falling in a recurrent fashion. In some scenarios, dreams of falling are a representation of some inferiority complex that the dreamer may be suffering from. These may also indicate fear of failing professionally or physically.

Some people only view dreams of falling as the dreamers opportunity where he is trying to make a choice in terms of giving in to sexual desires or not.

Most dreams of falling occur during stage one of sleep.

People who are spiritually inclined view dreams of falling as a sign that the dreamer is turning away from God and trusting man for guidance and advice.

DREAMING ABOUT CHEATING

Dreaming about cheating is really common and also immensely troubling. Some people view these dreams as a signal that they are being cheated on by their partners. This is however, almost never the case.

Now, cheating could be a real thing – however, you must remember that it can never make you psychic. Sometimes, your conscious mind may pick up certain signals that it may send to the subconscious mind. Things like your partner changing their dressing style for good or getting a new cologne may through the power of your subconscious mind manifest themselves as dreams about cheating.

A number of times, dreaming about cheating is not associated with your loved ones cheating on you. They are simply a manifestation of your own guilt and anxiousness. An example could be you dreaming about catching your partner red handed. Now, this could simply be an expression of you trying to hide your own shame and guilt.

Sometimes, dreams about cheating may not even point towards a relationship issue in real life. They may simply be a representation of how you feel about a particular issue and this could be any issue (not specifically related to your relationship).

You may dream about cheating if in real life you are intending to or have cheated in a particular test. Are you cutting corners at work?

Well, in this case too – you may begin to dream about cheating.

So, what does this imply?

This means that dreams are merely a representation of how you feel about a particular thing in real life or may be how you behave in real life.

Dreaming about cheating may stem from fear of failure at school, work and home. Sometimes fear is simply a measure of abandonment. A number of people who have seen their parents fight over trivial issues or witnessed parental divorces dream about cheating.

To wrap this up, it really does not matter who is cheating on you in your dreams. What really matters is how you take stock of your life, review your options and confront any issues that you are facing.

Always remember that dreams about cheating signify much more than a failed relationship. Look at every aspect of your life to arrive at a conclusion and then take informed decisions.

DREAMING ABOUT FAILING A TEST

Dreaming about failing in a test is one of the most common dreams experienced especially by students. These dreams imply loads of anxiety and fear associated with the dreamer's real life.

Now dreams about failing a test are not symbolic – they are generally a manifestation or representation of certain failed tests in the past or the present. Some students have never failed a test and are considered as good students. On certain nights, they may also dream about failing a test. This is because these students have set very high standards for themselves.

Such dreams are so intense that students even get to feel the hardness of their chair and the sharpness of their pencil. Sometimes, the test location or the language may not be familiar. In this scenario, students often dream about failing a test.

Sometimes, students dream about their pencils breaking or they falling short of time for the test. This clearly represents the dreamer's unpreparedness for the exam.

Sometimes, in their dreams, the dreamer can recollect the questions that he attempted or skipped in a particular exam. This also represents his fear of result, low self-confidence or heightened anxiety level.

Sometimes, dreams of fear of failing a test may also signify that that the dreamer fears that the people around him are judgmental about his abilities and personality.

Recurring dreams of failing may signify the need to reexamine your life and take a closer look at the goals that you have set for yourself. You may have set the goals too high and may now need to take a fresh look at them.

DREAMING ABOUT CRUSH OR CRUSHING

When you dream about crushing another person, it signifies tremendous pressure or stress over some decisions that you need to make

Sometimes people dream about a part of their body being crushed. This signifies that they are unable to fully express themselves in real life.

If you dream about having a crush on somebody, well... you may just be attracted to that person in real life. Dreaming about your crush simply denotes the level of infatuation that you have for that person. If you are constantly thinking about her or him during the day, then it can only natural to dream about them during the night.

Sometimes, you may begin to experience recurrent dreams about your crush. This is simply a representation of letting your crush know about your feelings for him or her. If you are really worried about the relationship, you may begin to experience recurrent dreams about your crush. This is a strong signal from the Universe that lets you know how talking to your crush can make things better for you. Even if they are disinterested, you get an opportunity to move on.

If you dream that your crush has died, it represents that your feelings for him or her are no longer as strong as they were. This could just be the universe's way of guiding you to move on.

Dreaming about another person having a crush on you is a symbol of how you view your own self – you are proud of yourself and hold yourself in high esteem.

You may even dream about a former crush. This points out to a specific period in your life and is a representation of how you were feeling then. This may also signify that a waking relationship is repeating the same pattern.

DREAMING ABOUT DATE OR DATING

Your need for self-awareness and self-discovery manifests itself through your dreaming about being on a date. This signifies that you are now getting to understand some hidden aspects of your own self and recognizing your hidden talents. It may also be a representation of your anxieties about dating or accepting some things in life. If you are really anxious or stressed out about a particular date that you have, then dreaming about that date could just be a 'rehearsal.'

A number of people who love their significant others get worried when they dream about dating two people at the same time. This simply indicates the passion in your own personal relationship. It does not imply that you wish to stray from your significant other. Such dreams can also be a manifestation of real life anxiety when it comes to maintenance of a relationship.

If you dream about a particular year, month or a date, you may be reminded of a special event that has occurred or is about to occur in your real life. You must also look at the section 'Understanding the hidden meaning of numbers' in order to correctly interpret what the date that you dream about suggests.

If you dream about being on a double date, you need to look at your real self closely. Is there a difference in the manner in which the world views you and how you view yourself? Dreaming about a double date may just represent the duality associated with your personality – you may be behaving in a different manner in front of the world and in reality may be a different person.

Another interpretation of dreaming about a double date is your need for togetherness and socializing.

DREAMING ABOUT ENGAGEMENT

Dreaming about getting engaged in order to get married is a symbol of your sexual desires. It may also signify your need for a stable relationship. Your desire towards commitment and security can be manifested through dreams about engagement. You may also be making an effort to resolve your feelings of loneliness in real life. This can be manifested through your dreaming about getting engaged.

A number of unmarried people dream about getting engaged. This is the universe's way of letting them know that they are now ready to take on any commitment.

Sometimes, you may get worried because you dreamt of getting engaged to your father. This is simply a representation of your quest for a father figure. It does not signify that you should or would marry your father. It is just a representation of your hidden desire to have a father figure in your life. Perhaps, you want your date to be as great as your father.

If you dream about breaking an engagement, you could be making some really hasty and unwise decisions in real life.

Some people dream about business engagements. This denotes their concern about their work. It may also indicate worry or opportunity in a particular work area.

DREAMING ABOUT YOUR EX

Are you currently experiencing similar feelings that you felt when you were with your ex? Is there someone in your life who makes you feel in a similar manner as your ex would make you feel?

If this is the case, you would naturally dream about your ex-husband/wife or ex-boyfriend/girlfriend. You may also dream that you and your ex are kissing/fighting with each other. Sometimes you may dream about you and your ex getting back together again. All this is indicative of the fact that there is someone in your life who makes you feel just the way your ex made you feel a few years back. This dream may just be the Universe's method of alerting you of similar behavioral patterns in your current life. You may simply be required to utilize the learnings from your past experience into your current relationship so that you do not repeat the same mistakes again. Alternatively, you may be required to think about the positive aspects of the relationship that you cherished with your ex so that you could implement the learnings in your present relationship.

Do you dream about getting back with your ex? Or maybe they wanting to get back with you?

You must understand that this is in no manner a manifestation of reality. It can even be triggered by a trivial fight in your present relationship.

Specifically dreaming about your ex husband or wife signifies that you are currently in a situation that you really do not want to be in. This could also mean that you are going through a similar situation or relationship and now this is making you feel uncomfortable and unhappy.

Dreaming about getting back with your ex-husband/wife can mean that you are subconsciously reiterating the same mistakes or patterns from your previous relationship into your present relationship. It means that you are making the same mistakes and reacting the same way, once again!

You may be missing some areas of your past relationship. This may lead you to dream about your ex missing you.

Sometimes, dreams about your ex missing you are triggered when you move on with your life. This is just a symbol that you have moved on with your life and your ex have lost their chance with you.

If you dream about your love's ex, it is suggestive of the fact that you are now committing the same mistakes that were committed by their ex. It may also mean that you are comparing yourself to the ex.

Dreams about your ex dying suggest that you must move on with your life as your feelings for your ex are completely dead. This is the universe's way of telling you that it is time to let go of the past and begin your new life.

Sometimes you may dream about your ex when you have neglected certain areas of your personality. This is a sign for you to acknowledge the situation, take control of your life and move on with what is best for you.

Sometimes women dream about their ex-boyfriends from childhood. This is suggestive of a free, non-complicated and less encumbered relationship. Such dreams take you back in time when you had not responsibilities and therefore romance and dating was spontaneous. It may also signify that your present relationship lacks freedom, excitement, youthfulness and romance. This is the universe's way of telling you that you need to bring these elements back in your life.

You may sometimes witness an ex-boyfriend hurting you in your dreams. This is a signal for you to move on with your life and simply forget the ex.

Do you miss being in a committed relationship? Do you want your ex back in real life too? In both these scenarios, you may dream about you craving for your ex-boyfriend's love. If your ex-boyfriend is advising you on the do's and don't's of a current relationship, it is a signal that your subconscious is trying to send to you. You do not want to repeat the same mistakes again!

Sometimes, as a result of our experiences from the past, we shield ourselves with a wall around us. We need to let go of the past and open up to our present situation and relationships. This is suggested through dreams about your ex massaging you. You do not have to be defensive now. You can get up, gather yourself together and bravely face the world.

Some women reflect on their past relationships to discover how complete they felt when they were with their ex. This leads to dreams about an ex-boyfriend proposing or giving them a ring.

This dream should never be confused with a longing to be with your ex. All it implies is that you have a need to be loved and cared for. It may also signify a beginning to something new and a final end to the not so great things in life.

Depending on the context of the dream, dreams about proposing may signify that you are now ready to move on with life. Since he is proposing to you, you possess the power to decide the fate of the relationship. You can choose to say a yes or a no.

If you dream about being gifted a stuffed toy by your ex, it signifies your need for a nurturing and reassuring relationship. This does not imply that you want your ex back. It simply means that you need more nurturing at the moment and may be indicative of the fact that you need to end a present immature relationship.

You may sometimes be having a tough time coming to terms with your break up. If this is the case, then it is not uncommon for you to dream about the hospitalization of your ex. This may also signify certain unresolved issues that need to be sorted out.

If you dream about your ex-boyfriend getting discharged from the hospital, your subconscious is simply giving you a signal that you need to now move on. If, in your dreams, your ex-boyfriend is dressed up in a suit inside the hospital, it is significant of initiation of the healing process.

Sometimes, women dream about walking away from their present relationship and moving hand in hand with their ex-boyfriend. This suggests that they are not satisfied with the relationship that they are into currently and that their present love interest does not match up to their ex-boyfriend.

If your ex is still emotionally attached to you, you may dream of getting kidnapped by him.

Men often dream about their ex-girlfriends getting pregnant. The interpretation of this dream depends on the context. If you have dreamt that the baby is yours, then this implies that your subconscious wishes to get back with your ex. In case your dream depicts that your girlfriend is pregnant and the baby is not yours, then it may indicate the relationship is over and that you have accepted this fact. This also suggests that in spite of ending the relationship, you have not stopped caring about her.

Have you ever seen your girlfriend's mother in your dreams?

This is indicative of the fact that you still have some unresolved issues with your girlfriend. Since your subconscious is reminding you about these unresolved issues, it is also coaxing you to approach her mother and get things settled between the two of you.

It is not uncommon for girls to dream about their present boyfriend's ex-girlfriend. This, however, reflects your own feelings of insecurity. You may still feel her subtle presence in your relationship and also wonder in case you match up to her. In real life, your insecurities lead you to make comparisons between your own self and your ex-boyfriend's girlfriend. This is never healthy for a relationship. Therefore, the dream is suggestive of taking specific actions that boost your self-confidence.

DREAMING ABOUT KISSING

Dreams about kissing are quite common, especially if you are anticipating your first kiss. In general dreaming about kissing signifies affection, love, harmony, tranquility, and contentment.

Sometimes, it may simply be the anticipation of feeling and experiencing your actual first kiss.

Dreaming about kissing is often representative of a person's first love and some fresh romance. This may be your subconscious telling you to inject your present relationship with some more love and romance.

Sometimes, you may be too involved in somebody else's personal life. In this case, you would dream about this somebody else kissing you or somebody else. This is an indication that the person you are too involved with needs some space.

If in your dream you are awakened just when about to kiss someone, it is an indication of you wondering how this someone really feels about you. You definite long for a relationship with this person but are not sure about the manner in which you can go about achieving it.

Heterosexual individuals often dream about kissing people from the same sex. This denotes self-realization and acceptance. It just indicates that you are acknowledging your masculine and feminine side. When you dream about kissing your own self, you are demonstrating self-love and self-confidence. You accept yourself fro who you are and are therefore kissing yourself.

Dreaming about kissing another person's hand or demonstrates respect, admiration and reverence. The same is true is you dream about another person kissing your hand.

Dreaming about kissing another person's foot signifies humility and respect.

Dreaming about kissing another person on the cheek is a symbol of adoration, friendship, courtesy, and/or respect. The same is true if you dream about another person kissing you on your cheek.

Dreaming about kissing a person's neck signifies uninhibited lust and passion. Dreaming about somebody kissing your neck also signifies the same thing. It is simply a sign that you are now ready to realize your physical desires.

Do you wish to experience the energy of love? Do you wish to enter into a physical relationship? Dreaming about kissing someone else's girlfriend or boyfriend indicates that you have this wish and are a little jealous of the happenings around you. It can also be looked as a way to awaken your passion. Sometimes, dreaming about kissing someone else's partner may indicate lack of integrity on your part.

Dreaming about kissing is often triggered by a major change in your present relationship and how far you have come from your past relationships. In this case, you generally dream about kissing your ex. This simply signifies that you want to reflect back on the positive experiences of the past and love the good times that you shared with your ex. Such dreams may be signals for you to re-evaluate your current relationship.

When you seek some intimacy or closeness in a relationship, you dream about kissing your close friend. This intimate closeness may not have any romantic interest for your friend. Such dreams will only denote adoration and respect for your friend.

When you kiss a stranger in your dreams, you only accept and acknowledge the repressed part of you. It may mean that you are in the process of discovering your own self.

Have you ever dreamt about kissing a celebrity? This indicates how strongly you desire success. You may want to look at this celebrity's life and evaluate the qualities that make him or her successful. You could then develop a specific action plan for yourself. You may also begin to dream about kissing a celebrity when you are overly obsessed with the celebrity. This demonstrates your fantasy about idealistic love and romance.

Dreaming about kissing an enemy are signs of betrayal, reconciliation or hostility with an angry friend.

There is a very popular saying – "this kiss of death".

If you dream about somebody trying to kiss you against your will, it may imply that this other person is trying to shove his beliefs, ideas, and opinions in your face. In real life, this person may be forcing you to do something that you do not really want to do. Dreaming about somebody trying to kiss you against your will could also mean that you are experiencing difficulty in accepting a particular part of your personality.

DREAMING ABOUT LOVE

Sometimes, intense feelings are carried over from a waking relationship. This is when a person almost always experiences dreams about loving someone or being in love with someone. This signifies that you are content with where you are and what you already have in life.

However, the interpretation of this dream is also based on the real life context. Sometimes, this dream may signify that you are making an adjustment and are not getting enough in your love life. The longing for acceptance and belongingness often leads to these dreams.

When you dream about another couple being in love or expressing their love for each other, it is a symbol of success that awaits you.

When you wish that your friend falls in love with you, or you develop feelings for your friend in real life, you may end up dreaming about them being in love with you.

Sometimes, this may also suggest that you love certain qualities in your friend and wish to incorporate them into your character.

If you dream about making love in public or may be at unusual and varied locations, it may just be a symbol of your non fulfilled sexual desires. This may just mean that you need to express yourself more freely.

Alternatively, such a dream may depict your perceptions about your own sexuality in the perspective of social norms. It is common to experience this dream if you are questioning your feelings about love, sex, gender and marriage.

Sometimes, you dream about your lost love. This is generally the case when your current relationship lacks excitement, romance, and freshness. This represents the fact that you are longing to get into an idealistic relationship.

Low self-esteem, fear, guilt, shame and lead you to dream about never being loved. This is simply a manifestation of your own unworthiness and requires a huge effort from your side in order to build self-confidence and self-acceptance.

Dreaming about your lover in your dream signifies self-worth, acceptance, and acknowledgement of your true inner value. It depicts that you are now assimilating aspects of the masculine and the feminine. As a result of this, you begin to feel complete and whole.

Sometimes, dreaming about your lover is a result of an unfulfilling relationship. This is when you dream about an ideal dream lover.

Dreaming about former lover is significant of certain unresolved issues regarding a specific relationship. It is a signal that your present relationship is asking you for solutions. You may be experiencing the same kind of issues in your present relationship.

Insecurity in present relationships may lead you to dream about being a part of a love triangle where you and one more person are in love with your partner. This is an indication that your attention or time is being divided in real life.

Dreaming about being in love with two different individuals implies that you are not entirely committed to your current relationship. Such dreams may also be a result of a strong emotional conflict where you are trying to find different parts of your own personality. It is all a part of discovering yourself.

DREAMING ABOUT LUST, INFIDELITY AND MAKING OUT

Dreaming about infidelity (either by you or someone else) signifies that there are unresolved issues of neglect and abandonment in a relationship. It may also mean that you are emotionally limited and need an outlet in order to express your feelings.

You may also begin to dream about infidelity if you are currently unsatisfied with you relationship. This may stem from guilt and shame or may be a result of your need for a more erotic sexual life.

You may often begin to dream about lust or that you are lusting after someone. This is demonstrative of your feeling of non fulfillness and may suggest an emotional void in your real life. It may also imply that you need practice some more self-control.

You may dream about people lusting after you if you think too highly of your own self. It is representative of an elevated sense of self-worth and self-esteem.

Dreaming about making out with someone demonstrates your fear of losing a particular relationship. It implies that you possess an intense desire to pursue a particular relationship, however the fear of jeopardizing the friendship is haunting you.

If this is not the case, then you may simply need to accept your relationship with the person and see if there are some parts of this persons character that you want to incorporate in your life.

CONCLUSION

I hope that this book has been able to provide you with a fair idea about your dreams. The function of the dream cycle continues to be a topic of debate till today. It is important to understand that dreams must be interpreted based on the context of the dream and the dreamer's real life situation. By the time you turn eight, you would have experienced at least 116,800 to 200,000 dreams. And evidence even suggests that the process of dreaming begins before birth! Now that's really fascinating!

THANK YOU

Before you go, I want to warmly say "thank you" from the bottom of my heart! I realize that there are many e-books on the market and you decided to purchase this one so I am forever grateful for that.

Thanks a million for reading this book all the way to very end!

If you enjoyed this book then I need your help!

Please take a moment to leave a review for this book after you turn the page.

This valuable feedback will allow me to write e-books that help you in your journey through life. And if you love it, please let me know.

Don't forget to get your Free Copy of "Superfoods"

>>awesomehabits.com/superfoodsbook<<

CPSIA information can be obtained at www.ICGtesting.com
Printed in the USA
LVOW04s1540130215

426956LV00015B/494/P